EURIPIDES

HEKABE

EURIPIDES
HEKABE

Freely translated from the Greek
by Robert Emmet Meagher

BOLCHAZY-CARDUCCI PUBLISHERS, INC.

for
Marilyn
Maribeth
Annemarie

ISBN 0-86516-330-8
Published by
BOLCHAZY-CARDUCCI PUBLISHERS, INC.
1000 Brown Street
Wauconda, Illinois 60084

Library of Congress Cataloging-in-Publication Data

Meagher, Robert E.
    Euripides Hekabe : freely translated from the Greek / by
Robert Emmet Meagher.
        p.   cm.
    ISBN 0-86516-330-8 (alk. paper)
    1. Hecuba (Legendary character)--Drama. 2. Trojan War--
Drama. I. Euripides. Hecuba. II. Title.
PS3563.E175E8 1996
882'.01--dc20   96-11963
                                                         CIP

FOREWORD

The dark turbulence and elusive complexity of ancient Greek literature are often bartered at a loss for something more simple and edifying. Translucent truisms emerge and speak for all that was Greek wisdom, truisms which fail to tell the whole truth: "It is better to suffer evil than to inflict it." "Nothing in excess." "Wisdom comes with suffering." Like ancient temples and statues, stripped of their once lurid paint and bleached by Christian commentary, the texts of the past offer limited yet luminous inspiration. To anyone still able and inclined to listen to the sublime, they speak with oracular authority. To everyone else, they speak past the point.

In 1968, campaigning in Indiana, Robert Kennedy was poised to address a massive crowd in Indianapolis, when he was told that Martin Luther King had been shot and killed. It fell to Kennedy to announce this fact and to address the outrage it would ignite. He tore up his written speech and said what came to him. What came to him was this:

> What we need in the United States is not
> division or hatred or violence, but love and
> wisdom and compassion toward one another,
> and a feeling of justice toward those who still
> suffer within our country, whether they be
> white or whether they be black. My favorite
> poet was Aeschylus who wrote: "In our sleep,
> pain, which we cannot forget, falls drop by
> drop upon the heart until, in our own despair
> and against our will, comes wisdom through
> the awful grace of God." So let us dedicate
> ourselves to what the Greeks wrote many years
> ago, to tame the savageness of man and to
> make gentle the life of this world.

Indianapolis was calm; but Chicago, for one, soon exploded. For a time, riot was the rule. Suffering does not always bring wisdom. Grief is not always humanizing. It did not take the assassinations of 1968 or the atrocities of what was Yugoslavia to teach us this. Greek tragedy is soaked with the counter-truth: suffering and grief are disfiguring and provoke hideous reprisals. Revenge is sweet, excess gratifying. These are truths most often excluded from the canon of Greek wisdom, ignored like the plays which house them, plays like Euripides' *Hekabe.*

Hekabe is living proof that powerlessness, like power, corrupts, and absolute powerlessness corrupts absolutely. Having endured blow after blow, loss after loss, she is well on her way to becoming an icon of innocent suffering, sculpted by pain, radiant in grief. Cradling her savaged son in her arms, Hekabe is on the verge of anticipating the Pietá. She is about to confirm the simple truth that it is always better to suffer than to inflict pain, a truth whose loyalties are at best suspect. This she refuses to do. Instead, to her own great horror, she learns another law and becomes as dark as what has been done to her. What she becomes and what she does are commended to us not for imitation but for hard thought; for the truth at hand is not as simple as we have been led to believe. We cannot count on suffering – our own or others' – to be ennobling.

Hekabe tells us something we need to know: that it is better to go dark in death than to go dark in life, that it is a curse to outlive our ability to affirm. Hekabe lives too long and suffers too much. She begs to have her life taken from her. Instead, she is propped up and made to go on, as if she were testing an ancient proposition, that suffering is humanizing, that fire purifies. In doing so, she finds her only strength in others like herself, in the solidarity of the oppressed, the consortium of women, dreaded by Agamemnon and despised by Polumestor, kings accustomed to having their way.

In the end, Hekabe lives only "to see a bit of justice done." It turns out to be poetic justice, eyes for eyes, teeth for teeth, briefly and deeply satisfying. Indeed, as the Chorus in Euripides' *Elektra* put it so plainly, "Justice can conduct itself shamefully." The *Hekabe* presents a spectacle of suffering, rage, and revenge, endured and enacted by women, who, as Euripides realized, suffer first and most from war. So long as we live in a world all but defined by violence, Euripides' *Hekabe* will offer compelling witness to the courage and solidarity of those who suffer most and a fierce challenge to the simplistic assurance that suffering is somehow for the better of us all.

R.E.M.
Amherst, Massachusetts

CAST

GHOST OF POLUDOROS
Youngest son of Hekabe

HEKABE
Queen of Troy

HANDMAIDEN
Attendant to Hekabe

CHORUS OF TROJAN WOMEN
Captive slaves

ODUSSEUS
King of Ithaka

POLUXENE
Daughter of Hekabe

TALTHUBIOS
Herald to the Greek army

AGAMEMNON
High king of the Greeks

POLUMESTOR
King of Thrace

SONS OF POLUMESTOR

GUARDS
Attendants to Odusseus, Polumestor, Agamemnon

HEKABE

The tent camp of captive Greek women on Thrace,
where the Greek army, returning from Troy,
has drifted ashore,
the sails of their ships now limp for lack of wind.
The ghost of Poludoros enters.

POLUDOROS

I have come from the grey haunts of hell.
I have come at the leave of loner-god Hades,
    lord of the lost and the damned.
I am Poludoros, last son to Hekabe, last heir to Priamos.
I was a guest in this land,
    sent off in secret to the safety of a friend's house.
My father saw the end approaching.
Troy would soon lie beneath the bronze tips of Greek spears.
Too young to bear arms, I might yet bear the family blood.
Surviving was to be my service.
I came here as no beggar from some spoiled city.
When I came here Troy's towers scraped the sky
    and I carried with me gold enough to pay my keep
        and a good deal more.
From friend to friend I was sent.
From Priamos to Polumestor,
    from Troy-king to king of horse-loving Thrace.
And I was treated accordingly,
    so long as Troy's walls were without breach
    and Hector without equal.
Just so long as that I flourished like a well-tended sprout.
But no longer.
For as soon as the soul of my brother Hector
    went dark in death,
    as soon as our sacred hearth grew cold,
    as soon as my father Priamos was butchered
        by the son of Akhilleus at the family altar,
            hewn long ago by Apollo himself,
    when my house fell,
    in that moment the bond of hospitality
        snapped like a twig.
And our family friend took off his mask.

Polumestor cut me down in greed,
    and threw me to the surf.
My protector slit my throat to tally up my gold.

Now I am beached over there,
    rolled up on shore by the sea's thousand hands,
    bathed in salt and foam.
No one weeps over me.
No one sees to my rites.
For three days I have drifted in the open air,
    watching for Greek ships from Troy,
    watching the arrival of my ill-starred mother.
Now, bereft of my body, I hover here,
    close over my sweet mother's head.
I have seen the Greeks sit idle by their ships
    sulking at the empty sails.
I have watched the ghost of Akhilleus appear
    astride his own tomb,
    and check the entire Greek army
        in their eager journey home.
I have listened to the son of Peleus lay claim
    to my sister Poluxene,
    as victim and trophy to mark his remains
        and to sweeten the bitterness of his death.
And he will have her, a gift from his old fellows.
Today is assigned by Fate to my sister's doom.

But today, mother,
    you will see two of your children as corpses,
    me and my ill-fated sister.
In quest of a grave,
    I will wash up at the feet of your servant.
I have prevailed upon the powers below
    to let this happen,
    so that you, Hekabe, might lay me to rest
        with your own aged hands.
I have longed for this and it shall be.

Now, I must vanish.
She comes from the tent of Agamemnon,
    unsettled by a dream she has had of me.

    Hekabe enters. She is supported by two attendants.

Oh mother, first a queen, now a slave,
    you are bent every bit as low as ever high you stood.
Some god jealous of exceptions makes you pay with grief
    for every joy you ever knew.

HEKABE

Walk beside me, women of Troy.
Stave up an old woman, once your queen,
    now another slave among you.
Here, take hold, lead my steps, bear me up or I fall.
I put my arm like a gnarled branch in your grip
    and push my useless feet to keep up with yours.
O light flashed from god!
O heavy cloak of night!
Why do I shudder at what I have just seen in sleep?
Why am I in dread over a mere dream?
O mother goddess earth,
    you who spawn the dark winged forms
        caved within our souls,
    I would scratch from my eyes
        this clinging vision come in night.
Call off these fiendish hounding images
    of my daughter and my son!
You gods who watch over this land, watch over my son.
He is my anchor, the last hope of our house.
He is in good hands.

But I am almost foreseeing something else,
    something unforeseen.
Never before have I known such clawing at my heart.
I shake all over without knowing why.
I need Helena the seer
    or my own prophetess-daughter Kassandra
    to read for me these runes
        burning themselves into my mind,
    and to tell me what it is I have seen.
There was a dappled fawn.
It clung to my knees in despair and I held it there.
But to no avail.
There was a fox too.
It drove its razor claws into the fawn
    and tore its flesh from between my fingers.
Whatever I still held was left behind.

Soaking in its own blood,
    the quivering fawn was dragged off.
There was no hint of pity shown.

And then a second vision came to me.
I saw the ghost of Akhilleus mounting his own tomb.
He wailed for a token of honor.
One of the war-sick Trojan slaves was his idea of a prize.
Gods, call off these omens. I am begging you.
Exempt my daughter from what by now is Fate.

The Chorus of Trojan women enters.

CHORUS

Hekabe,
We come to you in all haste,
Quitting the tents of our would-be lords.
A throw of the dice made us theirs,
Once our city fell to their spears.

Hekabe,
Our haste is not to lighten your grief,
But to tell what must be told.
What we bring is beyond all bearing.
You, it seems, are the last to know.

Hekabe,
The Greeks have met
And formed one mind on this:
Akhilleus is to have his way.
Your daughter is to be his prize.
A victim very to his liking.
Hekabe,
You know already how he mounted his tomb,
A ghost in golden armor,
And reined in the ready ships,
Bellowing like a maddened bull.

"Greeks, where do you think you are off to,
Leaving my tomb without its prize?"
These words swept over the crested host,
Like a storm at sea.

Hekabe,
Greek was set at odds with Greek.
Some would sate the lust of Akhilleus at any cost.
Others at the same expense
Would deny him his desires.

Hekabe,
There was sheer deadlock among them
Until one man sped to speak on your behalf.
No slight spokesman this,
Agamemnon,
Lord of lords among them all.

Hekabe,
To save his bacchant bride for his own bed,
Agamemnon made his case as best he could.
But then there rose against him
No less than the two sons of Theseus.

"Greeks,"
Spoke the two as if they were one,
"Do we owe more tribute to a slave's prowess in bed
Than to a fallen warrior's pride?"
These words brought the deadlock back.

Hekabe,
This battle of words swung from side to side
As evenly as a pendulum,
Until one wily man spoke up, Odusseus,
Sweet-tongued, slit-eyed liar.
"Greeks,"
He cried and brought silence
Like a shroud upon them all.
"Shall we slight the best of the Greeks
To spare our hands
Some slavewoman's blood?"

"Greeks,"
He went on catching every eye in his web,
"Shall we let tales be told to the gods below,
Tales of how we forget those who die for us,
Let them go below without their due?"

Hekabe,
Whatever needed to be said to sway the throng,
It came to his lips as if on call,
And now he comes to pry loose your brittle grip
From a daughter you cannot hope to save.

Hekabe,
Go to the temples, go to the shrines,
More to the point, go to Agamemnon.
Play the suppliant at his knees
Invoke every god in sight.

Hekabe,
Your entreaties are all that stands now
Between your hapless child
And a long sharp blade.
If you fail,
Your sweet girl will lie in a swelling pool
of her own dark rippling blood.

HEKABE

I am undone. Undone.
What kind of groans, how many screams do you prescribe?
It is over with me. Who is left of my house?
Who is left of my city to come to my side?
My husband gone. My sons gone.
What does that leave?
Where does someone with no one turn?
Is there a god or some other power likely to help?
Women of Troy, you bring the worst of all news.
Your words bring me to my brink.
What now could make me want to live?
There, a little further,
    help this ruin of a woman take a few more steps.

Child! Daughter! Your cursed mother calls you.
Come out and hear me.
Talk with me about these rumors bearing on your life.

Poluxene enters from the tent.

POLUXENE

Yes, mother? Mother, why do you cry out like this?

The panic in your voice has startled me like a skittish bird.
What is it?

HEKABE

Oh my baby.

POLUXENE

What? I already know it is something dreadful.
What is it?

HEKABE

I fear for your life.

POLUXENE

Mother, don't try to spare me.
Just tell me… no… no… I am afraid.
I'm shaking with fear, mother.
Why are you wailing?

HEKABE

My poor child, my poor, poor child.

POLUXENE

Mother, you'd best tell me what news you bring.

HEKABE

The Greeks have met in full assembly.
They voted.
They are going to sacrifice you on Akhilleus's tomb.

POLUXENE

Mother, how can your lips form such words?
Tell me what you are saying, mother.
My fear did not let me hear you.

HEKABE

What I am saying is the blackest of rumors…
    the Greek decree of what is to become of you.
They…

Hekabe breaks down, and Poluxene goes to her.

POLUXENE

My poor sweet mother.
You have endured so much.
Your life has become a wound that never heals.
What new outrage have they conjured up for you now?
I would have been a child to you,
    bringing whatever consolation
    a child might bring to her mother.
I would have been miserable with your misery,
    a companionship worth something.
But it seems even this will not be.
I hear you now.
I know what is to be.
You will see me dragged away,
    squalling like some young fawn blind with fear.
They will open my throat with one swift slice
    and I will bleed my way to hell.
But you, mother of sorrows,
    I cry your laments not mine.
I am the lucky one now.
Death turns out to be a blessing set against your woes.

Odusseus enters.

ODUSSEUS

Woman, by now you surely know
    the resolve of the Greek army.
But I will tell you all the same.
This is what shall be.
Your daughter will die spread across Akhilleus's tomb.
He has asked for her from death,
    and we have seen fit to give him what he wants.
We Greeks do nothing arbitrarily.
We came to this by vote.
I have been duly appointed to bring you this word
    and to take the girl away.
The son of Akhilleus will have the honor of presiding
    as priest of the sacrifice.

Have I told you all you wish to hear?
Then you know where you stand.
Don't indulge yourself with gestures of force,
    only forcing my hand.

Recognize your weakness and embrace your ills.
There is wisdom to be had in giving ground
  to what will happen anyway.

HEKABE

O gods!
Still another world of mine must fall apart.
Where will the wonted groans and tears come from
  this time?
I needed to die in Troy, but I could not.
Zeus would not take me.
Instead, in his largesse,
  he gave me more and more cursed strength.
God seals my cracks
  as if I were the last vessel in his fleet.
And yet I serve only to suffer always more and always worse
  than what I suffered last.
If slaves have any place at all to ask their masters "why?" –
  why you crack our hears beneath your heels
    like the dry shells of locusts –
  then I ask you: why must this be?

ODUSSEUS

Ask whatever you care to ask.
I have a few minutes.

HEKABE

I want to ask if you remember the time you came to Troy,
  a spy in a beggar's disguise, all rags and filth.
You played your part well.
Real tears filled your pleading eyes.

ODUSSEUS

O course I remember.
It's not the sort of thing you forget.

HEKABE

I should think not; for you were found out.
Helena recognized you.
She told me who you really were.
I was the only one she told.

ODUSSEUS

I remember well enough.
I was as good as dead.

HEKABE

At any rate you lost your pride.
You fell to your knees before me.

ODUSSEUS

Yes, and the hand I reached out to you
    was already growing cold at death's approach.

HEKABE

And what did you have to say then,
    when you were in my position… a slave?

ODUSSEUS

I found what words I could
    to talk my way out of death.

HEKABE

You talked your way out of nothing!
I spared you and sent you on your way.

ODUSSEUS

In any case, I'm very much alive today.

HEKABE

And you can stand there without despising your own words,
    you who owe your breath to me?
I gave you your life when it was gone,
    and you give me the greatest grief I can imagine.
You are the worst of a bad breed –
    you politicians, panderers –
    you pretend to focus the energies of a people
    and do no more than unleash your own greed.
I loathe you all.
I don't want to know you.
You forsake your friends
    to fawn over faceless crowds.

But tell me, politician, since you have a few minutes…
What neat case did you make for this blood-vote?
Just how did you propose a human sacrifice,
	when custom calls for cattle?
Or is it a matter of revenge – life for life?
If that is it, tell me.
How did you Greeks, who do nothing arbitrarily,
	indict my little girl?
How many of Akhilleus's wounds is she accused of inflicting?
How in god's sight did you pass over Helena?
That bitch's blood screams for spilling!
Akhilleus sailed to Troy on her account.
On her account he died.

But maybe all you want is looks. Is that it?
Did my daughter win a beauty contest?
You took your pick among slaves to give your horny ghost
	the kind of lay to silence his complaints?
But if it is loveliness you are after, don't shop in Trojan tents.
You Greeks already have Helena,
	uncontested queen of beauty.
And, as a bonus,
	Akhilleus ought to want to see her dead
		for all the grief she heaped on him.

So much for the logic of your case.
Now I make my own. Hear me.
I am asking only what I gave,
	when you asked the same of me.
I go to my knees. I reach out my hand.
I play the other part
	in a scene you say you remember well.
Don't take my child from me. Don't kill her.
Surely there has been enough killing.

She is the only joy I have left.
With her at my side, I have moments
	when I almost forget what I have been through.
She is my world…
	filling in for everything I have lost.
She is my solace, my nurse, my staff.
She guides my on my way.
Take her and you take everything!

The powerful do not do well to abuse their power.
No turn of fate fails to turn some day.
I know. I was once where you are now.
You see how much remains.

Akhilleus, look at me. Have pity.
Return to the Greek army
    and bend back their wills from this new resolve.
Show them what they are doing and its shamefulness.
When they tore us from our homes in Troy,
    they could easily have cut us down then and there.
But they took pity, spared us our lives and made us slaves.
That is where matters stand.
Your law is clear on this. Point that out.
To kill a slave or to kill a freewoman come to the same thing.
Murder!
Your word carries a lot of weight, for good or for ill.
They will heed you.

CHORUS

Human nature admits of many forms;
    but none so callous and remote
        as not to be touched by this woman.
Hekabe, your laments would bring tears from a stone,
    much less from a man.

ODUSSEUS

Hekabe, now it is for me to instruct you.
I have spoken with good will and good sense.
If I seem the villain, your wrath has made me so,
    twisting my words out of form.
You spared my life, granted.
I stand no less ready to spare yours.
That propriety is not in question.
Some things, after all, are sacred.

Your daughter... is another matter. She is called for.
I pledged her long ago to our most shining champion
    as soon as Troy would fall.
Troy, you know, has fallen, and my pledge stands.
Akhilleus, first among us, wants her with him dead.
She is the least we can do for him.

Among some other race this might not happen, granted.
Some people pay no more honor to the best and the bravest
    than they do to the least among them.
This is why their strength and spirit wane.
We Greeks possess the vision to measure worth
    and the heart to reward it.
And there was no man of greater worth than Akhilleus.
It is just that simple.
He was the fairest of all who gave their lives for Greece.
Woman, you tell me this: would there not be shame
    in revoking friendship from a corpse,
        even as it stiffens?
What would be left to say
    the next time we draw up our ranks for battle?
"Fight with all your hearts"?
Or "Best cling to life,
    seeing that in death you will be overlooked"?

Speaking for myself, in life I expect little enough;
    but in death I want my share of honor.
Honor done the dead never dies.
A good investment.

Woman, you say you have it bad.
Well, hear me.
We Greeks have our old women too who mourn their sons.
Too many Greek brides lie alone in cold beds,
    while their men lie in Trojan fields, colder still.
There is grief enough to go around.
So bear up.
And let us honor the best of our dead.
It is our right and our duty.
If we thought otherwise, we would know nothing,
    like you, barbarians, who forsake your friends
    and forget your dead.
And still you wonder why we are the ones to prosper!

CHORUS

This is what it means to be a slave:
    to accept the unacceptable,
    to endure whatever comes along,
        always without a word;
    to be too weak to think of doing otherwise.

HEKABE

Daughter, whatever arguments I assemble,
    they are blown away like chaff.
I speak to no avail.
What little time remains is yours
    to prevail if you can where I have failed.
Surpass the nightingale. Sing for your life.
Crawl if you must. Break his heart.
Even this man may have a crack in his wall.
After all, he has children of his own.
In you he may see them,
    and find pity he didn't know was there.

POLUXENE

Odusseus, I see you standing there at an angle,
    diverting your eyes.
You are a man in flight,
    afraid of being touched or of meeting eyes,
    afraid of a young girl.
Permit me to put you at ease.
In me your fear has no cause.
Don't worry, I am not about to call upon Zeus,
    hope of the hopeless.
I am going with you.
I have no choice but to die.
Yet, as it happens, to die *is* my choice.
It would be the mark of a base soul to resist you.
In doing so I would prove myself a coward.

What sense does it make for me to live now?

I was born a princess.
I was nursed on the highest of hopes,
    to be a bride for kings vying for my hand,
    to be the queen of the best among them,
    to live to a full age in his court.
I grew to be the acknowledged mistress
    of Troy's girls and women, conspicuous in every respect.
Mortality aside, I was a goddess.
And now I am a slave.
The name alone, so alien in every way,
    is enough to enamor me of death.

Am I to be an item for sale to coarse and brutal men,
    I, the sister of Hektor, sister to the princes of Troy?
Am I to know only harsh necessity,
       sweeping some man's floors,
       kneading his bread,
       making his bed
          from one weary day to the next?
Am I, the bride of kings,
       to let some crude slave from god knows where
       defile me in his filthy bed
         and call it love?
Never! I will take one last look at freedom
    and consign myself to hell.

Odusseus, lead me to my death.
I see no reason to trust or to hope
    that life will ever again be kind to me.

Mother, I am asking you not to say or to do anything
    aimed at breaking my resolve.
Join me, instead, in my will to die
    before I know a shame I do not deserve.
One who is unaccustomed to misfortune
    is bound to bear it badly.
Death for such a one is preferable to life.
Life without some grace is an effort not worth making.

CHORUS

Nobility of birth leaves its mark, conspicuous and singular.
But when the life that follows proves as noble as its birth,
    we have a wonder past all telling.

HEKABE

There is sheer beauty in your words, my child.
But it is a beauty bordering on despair.

Odusseus, hear me.
If Akhilleus must have his victim and you your repute,
    do not slay this girl.
Lead me instead to the site of this sacrifice.
Let me be its victim.
It would make more sense.

My son's arrows felled your chief.
I am the assassin's mother.
I ought not, it would seem, to be spared.

ODUSSEUS

Perhaps, old woman, there is sense in what you say.
But Akhilleus has his own mind in this matter.
He doesn't ask for you. He wants her.

HEKABE

Then at least take the two of us. Slaughter us together.
The earth and that demanding corpse of yours
    can drink my blood as well.
Surely Akhilleus will not complain
    if his cup is filled a second time.

ODUSSEUS

Her death will do just fine without any help from you.

HEKABE

I must die with my daughter! It can be no other way.

ODUSSEUS

You seem to think you are in a position to say what is to be.
Take another look!

HEKABE

I will cling to her like ivy to oak.

ODUSSEUS

Not if you have any sense.

HEKABE

I will not let you leave with her.

ODUSSEUS

And I have no intention of leaving without her.

POLUXENE

Mother, listen to me.

And you , Odusseus, try to understand a mother's feelings,
    natural enough under the circumstances.

O my poor, poor mother,
    please don't take on the whole Greek army.
You will only be torn away from me by arms
    twenty times your strength.
Then they will throw you to the ground
    and kick you around in the dust.
You are old. You will be hurt,
    and you will be dishonored.
Is this truly what you want? It is not what you deserve.
O mother, dear mother, give me your hand,
    and lean your head against mine.

Never again will I see the light of day.
Now for the last time I watch the sun
    trace its brilliant path across the sky.
I must form my last words.
Mother, you gave me life. Now I go below to darkness.

HEKABE

And I remain behind, in the light, a slave.

POLUXENE

I go to death unwed.
The time for bridal songs never came
    and now must wait forever.

HEKABE

Piteous and wretched, the two of us.

POLUXENE

I fall so far from you,
    to lie in some dark corner of hell.

HEKABE

O gods, what will I do? When can *I* die?

POLUXENE

I was born free, but I die a slave.

HEKABE

Fifty children, and I am alone. Not one is left to me.

POLUXENE

Do you have a message for Hektor or for father?

HEKABE

Tell them I am wretched, more than they imagine.

POLUXENE

Embracing Hekabe.

O gentle arms that held me, sweet breasts that nourished me.

HEKABE

O my baby, this fate of yours is all wrong.

POLUXENE

Good-bye, mother. Say good-bye to Kassandra for me.

HEKABE

"Good-bye." It has the wrong ring.
There is no word for this.

POLUXENE

Softly, to Hekabe alone.

Good-bye, dear Poludoros.

HEKABE

Also softly.

If he lives.
I am so shadowed I fear even for him.

POLUXENE

He lives.
He will be the one to close your eyes in death.

HEKABE

I am in death. I have not died,
    but my grief has already brought to me a kind of death.

POLUXENE

Shroud my head, Odusseus, and lead me away.
Even before I die the death you have designed for me,
  I have broken my mother's heart, and she mine.

O light of day, I am still able to turn to you,
  but only so long as it will take
  to reach the tomb of Akhilleus
  and the blade made sharp for me.

Odusseus covers Poluxene's head with her robe
and leads her out. Hekabe collapses.

HEKABE

I am faint. My legs give way.
O child, take hold of your mother.
Reach out to me. Give me your hand.
Don't leave me childless!
Women, it is over with me.
O gods what I wouldn't give to see Helena in her stead.
That one Spartan bitch, with her large, luring eyes,
  dragged thriving Troy to ruin.

CHORUS

Listen, listen, listen, listen, listen.
Winds of the sea,
The wine-dark waters shimmer at your approach.
Even to the tips of shore-side cliffs,
You waft the scent and tang of the salt-soaked sea.
You fill the long-limp sails with hope
And send the scudding ships to shores unseen
Save in the pining dreams
Of war-sick, homesick Greeks.

Listen, listen, listen, listen, listen.
Winds of the sea,
You fill your lungs to send us swiftly on our way.
But where will you lift these lost lives of ours
And set us down to stand for sale?
Where will this blind journey end,
So we might begin to spill out our lives in slavery
Like wasted wine
From cracked cups?

Listen, listen, listen, listen, listen.
Winds of the sea,
You carry in your breath a thousand cries.
You moan with a grief
We know well.

O children charred in ashen Troy,
O men sent to hell in your sleep,
At least you know a kind of rest
While our end lingers like a dying lamp.

Talthubios enters from the Greek camp.
Hekabe is lying prostrate on the ground.

TALTHUBIOS

Women of Troy, where might I find Hekabe,
    once your queen?

CHORUS

She is only right there, Talthubios, lying in the dust,
    shrouding her head in her cloak.

TALTHUBIOS

O god, what am I to say?
That you watch over our lives, solicitous and caring?
Or that we are fools to believe in a breed of provident gods
    when blind chance alone walks, or drags,
        us through our days?
This woman, was she not queen of gold-laden Troy?
Was she not wife of long-blessed Priamos?
Now, what is left of Troy grovels under Greek spears.
And the queen… she is a broken slavewoman,
    older even than her long years,
    without strength or child of her own
        to lift her to her feet;
    without pride or purpose
        to raise her head from the dust.
It is almost too much to believe or to bear.
I too am old, and I hope to god I die
    before I fall prey to such a shameful state.

Rise, lady, lift your face, so wan and weary,
    and stand on your feet.

HEKABE

Who is it who will not leave me be?
Whoever you are, why do you disrupt my grief?

TALTHUBIOS

I am Talthubios. I run errands for the Greeks.
Poor lady, Agamemnon has sent me to tell you...

HEKABE

Interrupting.

...that the Greeks want my life too?
That I am to die with my daughter?
O sweet man,
    I welcome you and your words.
Here, give me your hand. I am in a hurry,
Take me there.

TALTHUBIOS

You do not want my hand. I can lead you nowhere.
I have come to see if you will bury your daughter.
She is dead.
The army and the generals want you to see to her rites.

HEKABE

What am I to say?
Is that what you've come here to tell me?
That I cannot die with my daughter;
    and even worse that...?
    O my child, torn from these arms... you...
You are dead. Dead!
With you... all of my children... dead!
I am cursed!

Confronting Talthubios.

How did you do it?
Was there any respect given her?
Or did you go about your work savagely.
Tell me, old man.
Say what there is to say, whatever the pain involved.

TALTHUBIOS

Lady, I am a compassionate man.
I raise no walls against my feelings.
You are asking me to pay a second time in tears
    for your sweet daughter's death.
And so it must be.
I wept not long ago, watching her die.
And I shall weep again now,
    in the telling of that dark event.

The entire Greek army was gathered there
    at the tomb of Akhilleus,
    waiting to see your daughter die.
The son of Akhilleus took Poluxene by the hand,
    led her through the ranks of men
    and stood her on the burial mound itself.
I was there, very near to her.
When she was in her place, a cordon of handpicked guards
    closed in around your girl,
    in case she might decide to run for her life.
Then, taking in his hand a pure-gold cup,
    brimming with wine,
    the son of Akhilleus held it high,
        to pour a libation to his dead father.
Next he looked to me
    to summon the Greek throng to silence.
I took a step or two nearer and then,
    circled by that vast assembly, I cried out:
    "Greeks, silence! Silence in the ranks! Be still."
At once a hush swept over the Greeks, and he began to pray.

"Akhilleus, son of Peleos, Father,
    receive these libations, poured in propitiation,
        to raise up your spirit.
Crawl near and drink this gift
    from your son and your fellows,
        the gift of a virgin's blood, dark and pure.
Akhilleus, Father, be gracious to us.
Throw loose the ties that bind our ships to port
    and favor us all with fair journeys home."

These were his prayers, and he was joined in them
    by the whole army of the Greeks.

Then, his hand fitted itself to the hilt of his sword,
    and he slid it, gleaming gold, from its sheath.
With barely a nod from him,
    the guards circling the young girl
        closed in to seize her.
Yet before they could lay a hand on her, she cried out.

"Wait! Troy-sacking Greeks, not one of you touch me!
I am a free woman, and I will die that way!
Freely I offer my throat to your blade.
Untie my hands. I have no need of your constraints.
I said untie my hands! I shall die a free death.
All of you, stand off!
I go down among the dead the daughter of a king.
I am no man's slave, and I will not die like one."

With one voice the army roared its support.
And lord Agamemnon, mightiest among them,
    stepped forth and spoke to the guards.
"Untie her hands and let her be."
These were his words. They were done at once.

Then Poluxene, her hands now free, took her robe
    and tore it from her shoulders to below her waist,
    leaving bare her soft unblemished breasts.
She was to the eye the loveliest of statues, and more.
Then she lowered herself to her knees
    and knelt before the throng of Greek men.
These were her words, strong and boldly spoken.

"See here, man, if it is in my breast
    you wish to plant your blade, the way is ready.
Or if it is across my throat
    you think to slash your steel, here,
    I lean back my head to make it easy for you."

Torn with pity, the son of Akhilleus
    cut her deep and clean below the chin
    as her breath and blood burst from a single slit
    and spewed her life over the earthen mound.
Even as she swooned in death, she fell in modest form
    and covered from the eyes of men
        what was not theirs to see.

Lady, I have honored your request
   and told you what there is to tell.
This is what I heard and saw.
And now I see in you, of all women, a mother
   at once profoundly blessed and cursed unspeakably.

CHORUS

Some deep well of suffering
   is sunk within the house of Priamos.
Its dread dark waters seep within the soil of Troy.
Such is our lot to which the gods have yoked us.

HEKABE

O my child,
I need to confront the evils hounding me on every side.
But they are too many and too insistent for me
   to cope with them.
If I would turn to one, another cries out for my care.
I seem set upon some pitiless course of blow after blow,
   without respite.
How am I to cauterize my mind of you and your savage end,
   to forget and spare myself these groans and grief,
   which for all I know may never end?
All this I could not bear
   were it not for the tale this man has told of how
   you shone even beneath the shadow of your doom.

Strange the force of chance and fate
   over the fruits of the earth.
Even barren soil will harvest well when blessed from above.
And the richest soil throws up unwanted fruit,
   if starved of its own needs.
Not so with us. We hatch our deeds within,
   good from good, evil from evil.
We are without excuse for what we do.

Talthubios, go to the Greeks and tell them
   no one is to touch my daughter.
Curiosity will bring crowds,
   and I want them far from her.

       Talthubios leaves,
   and Hekabe turns to her handmaiden.

HEKABE

Old companion, do this for me.
Take a pitcher and go to the sea.
Dip the vessel into the brine and bring it brimming here,
 so that I might pour it over my daughter's corpse
 and give my girl her last bath.
Then, when I have washed away the filth of death,
 I shall lay her out as befits an unwed bride of Hades,
  a virgin spoiled in hell.
But how am I to do this? I have nothing that I need.
I must make do with what I can collect
 from other women in the tents.
Some of them may have secret spoils,
 which they managed to thieve
  from their own homes in Troy.

   The Handmaiden leaves.

Troy!
Home once so blessed.
You used to overflow with beautiful things
 and beautiful children.
Priamos… you and I…
 a worn old woman, mother of your children,
 how have we come to this?
How has everything come to nothing?
Even our spirit is broken in two.

All our vanity
 is vanity.
Our private wealth, our public honors,
 all come to nothing.
All that we turn over in our hearts
 and toss about upon our tongues
 comes down to this:

There is no more to be hoped for
 by anyone
 in any life
  than to elude ruin
  one day at a time.

   Hekabe enters the tent.

CHORUS

The roots of whatever happiness I knew
Were hacked and cut to death
The day Troy's comeliest prince
Took axe to towering pine
And shaped himself a ship.
Sown was the seed of my undoing
When pointed Trojan prows
Rammed the soft white surf
And set themselves to sea.
All this to fetch one woman from her bed,
Helena, sight of all sights
Beneath the seething sun.

Our avalanche of ruin began
With one small slip of soul.
One young man's unknowing,
The folly of a single fool,
Sufficed to doom us all.
In a never-ending storm of pain,
We watched iron-wielding rage
Hack apart our lovely sons
And redden the River Simois.
To survive all this is now to sit within those tents
And to keep open with our thoughts
Wounds that never close.

The Handmaiden enters, followed shortly afterward by two
of the Chorus carrying a bier and a covered corpse.

HANDMAIDEN

Women, our queen wears a crown of sorrow.
In this she is without rival or peer.
Her misery is beyond all measure.
Where is our lady now?

CHORUS

Why do you ask... and in that manner?
Already I dread your news. What is it now?

HANDMAIDEN

Hekabe must find room for still another grief.
O gods, how can I lighten the weight of these words?
I fear to crush her.

CHORUS

Look. She is coming now from her tent.
It seems she is in time for whatever it is you bring.

HANDMAIDEN

Lady, what can I say?
You are accursed beyond description.
You are a perished queen,
    no matter how your life lingers on.
Like an egg sucked dry,
    your existence is a shell about to crack.
Nothing is left to you.
Not your city, not your spouse, not your children.
Nothing is left but life's empty gestures.
Give any animal a violent enough end,
    and it will go on moving all the same for a while.
I fear we are no different.

HEKABE

I find your words offensive, but true enough.
In any case, you tell me nothing new.
But why have you brought my daughter's body here?
I was told the Greeks were making ready a pyre for her.

HANDMAIDEN

My lady, there is more to come.
After all this, you still do not know the worst.

HEKABE

No! Gods, no… no!
Tell me you don't cover there the sweet face
    of my god-struck child, Kassandra.

HANDMAIDEN

Kassandra lives. But your grief has cause.
O lady, come. You must see a sight beyond belief.

*The handmaiden draws back the shroud to reveal
to Hekabe the corpse of her last son, Poludoros.
At the sight of her dead son, Hekabe begins to groan
from a black and bottomless depth
which she inhabits now for the first time.*

HEKABE

Aoaoaoaoaoaoaoao… aiaiaiaiaiaiaiai…
My son… my son… my darling son!
Safe… in a friend's house… I lose even you.
I am no more.

Child… my child… aiaiaiaiaiaiai…
I have outlived the world I knew. I think strange thoughts.
My blood learns another law.
Why should I not give way to powers as dark
      as what I have become?
Child, my child… how? How can this be?
What power, what fate, what fiend
      did this to you?

HANDMAIDEN

My lady, I know no more than you.
I found him in the surf.

HEKABE

In the surf? Drowned at sea and washed ashore?
Murdered?

HANDMAIDEN

All I know… I found him sliding with the tide
      overlaid with kelp and scum.
It was like an awful dream.

HEKABE

A dream… my dream!
I see it now… those dark, winged forms…
      over you, my son, dead, even as I dreamed them.

HANDMAIDEN

What are you saying? Murdered?
Do you see in your dream who killed him?

HEKABE

Our friend, his protector, for gold and nothing more.

HANDMAIDEN

I can't believe my ears.
Poludoros slain to feed one man's greed?

HEKABE

My mind falls blank on such a deed.
He tossed away friendship like a used match.
He is the worst of men.
See what a hellish mess he made of my darling boy.
How many thudding blows does it take
    to hack out the life of a child?
I see each one of them now in his mangled flesh,
    and feel them as my own.

CHORUS

You are singled out, my queen, for suffering.
Some demon god must hold a heavy grudge
    against you and all you love.

Look, it is lord Agamemnon.
He is coming our way.

Agamemnon enters.

AGAMEMNON

Hekabe,
    why do you wait to bury your daughter?
I was told that all was ready for her rites.
Your delay seems strange to me. What keeps you?
There, behind you, what corpse is that,
    wrapped in a Trojan cloak?
Did one of the aged women die in this heat?
Tell me, who is it?

Hekabe says nothing.

Your silence disturbs me. You are hiding something.
Unlike your daughter, I have no psychic skills.
I cannot hear what you fail to say.
But why should I care who this is, if you do not.
One more Trojan dead alters very little.

Agamemnon turns to leave.

HEKABE

Lord Agamemnon, wait. Please!
I beg you, wait and hear me.

Lowering herself to her knees
and grabbing hold of Agamemnon's cloak.

I must ask you something.

AGAMEMNON

What is it, woman?
If you want your freedom,
    I give it to you without the asking.
It is a slight matter.

HEKABE

Yes, it is a slight matter. Not so with what I ask.
I want your help.

AGAMEMNON

My help? With what?

HEKABE

I seek revenge on one who well deserves it.

AGAMEMNON

On whom? For what?

HEKABE

You will know all you need to know, my lord,
    if you look under that shroud.

Agamemnon walks to the corpse and bends over it.
He hesitates.

HEKABE

Please!

Agamemnon uncovers the corpse and studies it briefly.

AGAMEMNON

A young man who came to no good end.
But this tells me nothing.

HEKABE

He is my son.

AGAMEMNON

How? Which of your sons is he?

HEKABE

No one of those that died for Troy.

AGAMEMNON

You bore others besides those?

HEKABE

Only one, my youngest... born for nothing.
You see what remains of him.

AGAMEMNON

I am grasping none of this.
Where was this boy when Troy fell?

HEKABE

Fearing for our last son's life,
    my husband sent him away.

AGAMEMNON

Where to?

HEKABE

Here to Thrace, where he was found dead.

AGAMEMNON

You sent him to Polumestor, king of Thrace?

HEKABE

Yes, with gold enough to keep him well.

AGAMEMNON

Then who did this, and why?

HEKABE

Our family friend, for gold. Now you know it all.

AGAMEMNON

Poor woman, there seems to be no end to your woes.
You think Polumestor slew your son in greed
    for one more chest of gold?

HEKABE

I know as much.
When Troy fell, he had nothing to lose,
    and a sum of gold to gain.
One thing is clear. It caused him no great pain.
His mind was made at once,
    and as quick the deed was done.

AGAMEMNON

Who found the corpse and brought it here?

HEKABE

This woman, my companion, saw him in the surf,
    washed ashore as flotsam.

AGAMEMNON

Then you are right.
Polumestor, his protector, cut your son down
    and flung him in the sea.

HEKABE

To float as bloody bait, luring demons from the deep.

AGAMEMNON

Woman, I pity you
    and how your grief must dredge your soul.

HEKABE

I died of grief some time ago.
What you see now is something else.

Agamemnon, hear me out, please!
Then, if you dismiss the charge I bring,
    I will have no more to say.
But if you judge me sorely wronged,
    I will call on you to help in my revenge
        on the most impious of men.

AGAMEMNON

You may go on, Hekabe. I will listen.

HEKABE

That man, defying gods above and gods below, betrayed
    every sacred bond between fellows and friends.
He ate at our table, called himself our friend,
    gave every warrant for our trust.
And then, given one ripe moment for his greed,
    he thought new thoughts,
        as if all the rest had been a dream.
He saw his chance and sent my son to hell,
    without the bother of a burial.
The sea would serve as well as any tomb
    for what to him was mere debris.

I know my place. I am a slave,
    as are these other women of Troy.
And slaves are weak.
But even the gods, in all their awful strength,
    are accountable to law.
There is right and there is wrong. No god can alter this.
And it is wrong to slay a guest.
This much, slave though I be, I know for sure.
Deny this and there is nothing left
    but an endless night of blind desires.

Agamemnon, you are not a god, but you are strong.
And, like a god, you too are ruled by law.
Do not turn away from me.
There is no escape from what I say.
Pity me and punish him.
It is his due; and it is mine to ask.
Look at me.
I have nothing left but this:
    to see a bit of justice done.

Agamemnon appears unmoved by Hekabe's words.

I sense I have failed as yet to find the mark
    and strike your heart.
Think then of your long nights of love in bed
    beside my girl, Kassandra, sister of the slain.
Is there not some debt or bond incurred in love's embrace?
There is no grace shown to mortals
    sweet beyond the charms of love.
I am the mother of your love.
He was the brother of your gladness.
Do right by him, and you do right by Kassandra.

Agamemnon remains unmoved.

All that now remains for me to do is to plead.
I beg you, peerless lord,
    you who are a light to your fellow Greeks,
        give way to my request.
Help an old woman, wronged beyond belief,
    to get her revenge.
It may be I am nothing to you.
Even so, justice is the work of noble men.
Prove yourself the man you are,
    and do not shirk your calling.
Bring evil home to roost.
Consign the wicked to their own harvest.
Destroy the fiend who killed my son!

CHORUS

Strange how things turn out.
Our lives are many-sided dice,
    picked up and thrown again
        by powers we never grasp.
Today's friends are tomorrow's foes.
Love and hate are back to back.
Only law will hold us to our course,
    when all else shifts and turns
        and shows to us a strange face.

AGAMEMNON

Hekabe, how can I do otherwise
    than pity you, your son, and your misfortune?
The gods, sheer justice, and my every inclination
    argue on your behalf.

The case is clear.
Polumestor is a villain,
    and you should have your way with him.
No revenge would be too dark for such a man.

You must see by now I am a compassionate man,
    not unfeeling toward your pain.
I have placed myself in your position
    and understood your plight.
Now I ask the same of you.
I have no doubt I would ally myself with you,
    if I were only free to do just that.
But I am not.

Can you look at things another way
    and see with Greek eyes for a change?
Whatever I might do on your behalf,
    to see your vengeance through,
    will seem to my own men
        a private favor done to please my mate.
Here is where the trouble lies.
All that Polumestor did to earn your hate
    would bring applause where I come from.
To the Greeks he is a friend.
And, when he kills a prince of Troy,
    he is all the more a friend.
Here we have no common ground
    for the law of which you speak.

In short, it comes to this.
In me you have a man
    who wants to take your cause and treat it as his own.
But I must be slow to rouse my fellow Greeks,
    very slow indeed,
        no matter what the rush in your regard.

HEKABE

Agamemnon, if you are as constrained as you describe
    I wonder if there is such a thing as freedom,
        save among the gods.
We mortals all are slaves, you as much as I.
We are blind in our desires
    and fail to see beyond our fears.

Our masters may well vary,
    but their yoke is the same.
You, a lord, allow a common crowd to lord it over you.
You say you fear what they might think,
    if you make common cause with me.
But this is one fear you may set aside,
    one constraint you need not heed.
If you will be a partner in my plot,
    you need not be a party to the deed.
What I ask is very small.
When the Thracian fiend falls prey to my designs,
    there may be Greeks inclined to give him aid.
You are a clever man and you will surely find a way
    to keep such meddlers far from me and what I do,
        without disclosing any common pact we've made.
Obstruct your fellow Greeks,
    give me the few free moments that I need,
        and I shall see that all is done to suit
        this man-turned-savage-beast.

AGAMEMNON

These are big words coming from a woman, Hekabe.
Just how do you propose to do what you describe?
I doubt your aged arm could lift a sword like this
    much less wield it with the speed you'll need
        to slice apart a man of half your years.
Poison serves a woman's anger best,
    unless she has a man to do her killing for her.
And you have no one at your side,
    no manly arm to raise against your foe.
You are alone in what you plan to do
    and thus seem doomed to fail.

HEKABE

Agamemnon, your lordly eyes are not as keen
    as one might think.
You see clear past the point in this affair,
    and overlook the power that is mine.
You may be right in claiming that a woman's arm
    is no likely match for manly force.
But I am not *a* woman. I am many. *We* are many.
You say I am alone in what I do,
    and in saying this you prove yourself the fool.

There are many women in those tents,
    who are not fond of men who slay their sons.
I am not alone.

AGAMEMNON

You mean our slaves… Greek hunters' prey?

HEKABE

Can you look at things another way,
    and see with women's eyes for a change?
What you see may be a mask worn at our discretion.
You know us not at all.

AGAMEMNON

I know that women are weak.

HEKABE

In force of arm, I will not quarrel,
    one to one you men prevail.
But when we count our common strength
    we soon add up to one of you.
The rest is craft,
    and there we women have no peers.

AGAMEMNON

I mistrust the power you describe.

HEKABE

You may trust to find us equal to our task.
We have our precedents for what we do.
Did not women slay the sons of Aiguptos
    without the help of men?
And how did Lemnos come to have no men?
Murdered one by one with weakness you dismiss!
I will say again what I have said. Leave this to us.
All I ask of you is safe passage for this woman
    through your ranks.

Agamemnon nods his assent,
and Hekabe turns to her handmaiden.

HEKABE

Go to Polumestor.
Tell him that Hekabe, once queen of Troy,
  summons him, and his sons as well,
  to come here, to me, for covert reasons,
    cogent none the less for everyone concerned.
If he wonders how his children figure in my scheme,
  say no more than this:
  They too must know the secret that I bear.

The Handmaiden leaves, and Hekabe turns to Agamemnon.

Agamemnon, I ask one thing more.
Delay the burial of my girl,
  so that brother and sister may share a common flame
  and know each other's touch
    when they lie side by side beneath a single mound
    of this foul Thracian soil.

AGAMEMNON

It shall be as you have said.
With sails as limp as ours are now,
  we Greeks are going nowhere,
  and can delay as suits your wish.
As for what you undertake, I wish it well.
You are not alone to gain,
  when justice finds its way on earth.
It is a common not a private thirst,
  which you set out to quench.

Agamemnon departs and Hekabe returns to her tent.

CHORUS

Women of Troy,
We belong to a city sacked
And brought to ruin.

Like a deafening, darkening locust-cloud,
Invading Greeks swarmed across our plains
And camped outside our gates.
From that day on we spent our lives
In the tightening coils of a viperous foe.

Our ten years of bitter siege
Were an unabating storm
Of pain and sorrow.

Women of Troy,
We shall never forget the fateful night
The coiled serpent struck.
Deceived into thinking the Greeks were gone,
A delirious city danced and feasted and drank its fill
Deep into the night.
Spears were hung again high upon the walls
And warriors went to bed without their swords.
Even in the tallest towers mounted on the city's walls
Thoughts of Greeks at last were gone,
And weary watchmen slept.

Women of Troy,
We were the last to bed that night
In our city glad with peace.
We stood naked before gold-glistening mirrors,
Combing from our hair and from our hearts
The snarls of bygone strife.
But then the night was rent in two
And all its demons flooded in.
We heard the shouts of hateful Greeks
Pouring through our streets
Like a poisonous plague.

Women of Troy,
We covered ourselves and fell to our knees,
While our husbands leapt for their spears.
In seconds we moved from peace to war
But even those seconds were too slow.
We watched our husbands die without a fight,
Swallowing Greek spears and crying to us
With mouths of blood.
With our eyes turned back to Troy in flames
We were herded into ships
And blown across the sea.

Women of Troy,
We have nothing now but our memories
And our anger.

Our souls are the embers of a smouldering Troy
And we must preserve its flame.
With every exiled breath we breathe,
In a land and a life no longer ours,
We summon rage.
A curse upon Helena and her love.
A curse upon all Greeks
And their friends.

During the last lines of the Chorus,
Hekabe emerges from her tent, as Polumestor enters
with his two small sons and several guards.
Hekabe does not acknowledge him.

POLUMESTOR

Dearest Hekabe,
    wife of my beloved friend Priamos,
        may-he-rest-in-peace,
    at the very sight of you tears well up in my eyes…
    for Troy…
and now for your lovely daughter's tragic end.
We live in dark times.
Where can you put your trust these days?
It's all we can do to keep our honor intact, much less…
Anyone of us can be on top of things today,
    and ruined tomorrow.
The gods can make a mess of any life… and will!
The best laid plans…

I suppose it's all to bring us to our knees,
    as if life makes some deeper sense down there.
But it doesn't do any good to go around moaning
    about what's over and done with.

My good lady, I sense your anger.
Forgive me, and try to understand.
As king of Thrace, I have many responsibilities,
    and some of them take me far afield.
I could not have come to you any sooner than I have.

HEKABE

Old and dear friend, you misread my anger…
    not anger at all.

It is shame that bows my head,
    shame that I a queen should fall so low.
When you last saw me, I stood wrapped
    in all the splendor this poor life may briefly offer.
And now you see for yourself what has become of me.
It is you who must forgive me;
    for I cannot raise my eyes to look you in the face.
Take this as no sign of my ill-will, my friend,
    but only of my shame.

POLUMESTOR

I understand, Hekabe, give it no more thought.
But now, tell me, what more can I do for you?
Your servant spoke of some new urgency.

HEKABE

Yes, there is something I would share with you…
    and your sons… in privacy…

Staring toward Polumestor's guards who stand nearby.

    if that is to be had.
Do you think we can be alone?

POLUMESTOR

To his guards.

You may leave.
I am alone… with a friend.
I will be safe here.

His guards leave, and Polumestor turns to Hekabe.

Now, you must tell me how I can use my good fortune
    to be of some help to you in your affliction.
Think of what I have as yours.

HEKABE

You are very gracious, just as I remembered you.
But first, my thoughts are of my son, entrusted to your care.
Tell me, Polumestor, is he well?

POLUMESTOR

He could not be better.
He is your one cause for joy.

HEKABE

Dearest friend,
    you have told me what I so sorely needed to know.
Knowing this much, I can go on.

POLUMESTOR

But now there must be more that you would have of me.

HEKABE

Yes, of course there is.
Yet I want to know more of my son.
Does he speak of me?

POLUMESTOR

He speaks of little else.
If it were not for my firm hand,
    he would be here now.
He wanted to come to you in some disguise.
I thought it best to keep him out of sight.

HEKABE

And the gold… is it in your hands?

POLUMESTOR

Safe within my vaults.

HEKABE

Best keep it there.
That much gold can bring forth greed.
I trust it would not tempt a friend.

POLUMESTOR

My life is full with what I have.

HEKABE

Yes, how could it be otherwise?
Now, do you know why I needed to see you and your sons?

POLUMESTOR

Not at all. We are waiting to find out.

HEKABE

Dearest Polumestor, I intend to be as good a friend to you
    as you have been to me...
        to return favor with favor.

POLUMESTOR

You needn't think in such terms.

HEKABE

O, but there are no others for a woman in my place.
There were secret stores of ancient gold
    belonging to the house of Priamos ...

POLUMESTOR

And this concerns me and my sons?

HEKABE

Indeed, for you are a man of honor...
    one of the last, it seems.

POLUMESTOR

But why did you want me to bring my sons?

HEKABE

I have more to say of this gold of mine.
And it is best that they too should hear it all,
    in case anything untimely should befall you.

POLUMESTOR

I see your point.
This war has taught us all a cunning
    we never knew we'd need.

HEKABE

Speaking for myself, I know this to be true.
But tell me, do you recall where Athena's temple
    once stood in Troy?

POLUMESTOR

The gold lies there?

                    Hekabe nods assent.

POLUMESTOR

Will I find a marker of some sort?

HEKABE

A black slab of rock jutting up from the earth.

POLUMESTOR

Is that it? Is the entire family treasure hidden there?
Or is there more besides?

HEKABE

It is all there… save a bag of priceless jewels,
    which I carried in my cloak from flaming Troy.
I cannot keep them hidden long.
Will you take them now and keep them safe?

POLUMESTOR

You have them here, now?
Are they concealed beneath your cloak?

HEKABE

They are well hidden in my tent.

POLUMESTOR

You keep them here, with Greeks on every side?

HEKABE

Our tents belong to us.
In that small sphere, they leave us captive women
    to our own devices.

POLUMESTOR

You think it safe within your tent?
There are no men inside?

HEKABE

No men. Only women.
Come, be my guest, as my son is yours.
I have a debt to pay.
You cannot begrudge me this.
Come quickly. We may not have much time.

The Greeks are keen to launch their ships
    at the first breath of homeward winds.
Then, after we are done,
    you will want to go at once and join my son.

Polumestor enters with his sons into Hekabe's tent.
The Handmaiden and the Chorus follow Hekabe into the tent.

CHORUS

King of Thrace, all debts come due,
Even for a man who wears a crown.
Once you thought the gods too slow
To catch you in your evil deeds.
But now you know
How swift the gods can be.
Always in the end, evil and ruin
Lie side by side.
You may think to steer a private course
Free of every rock and shoal.
But then you strike the unforeseen
And your once sound ship
Drinks the sea beneath your feet.
What man is equal to the ocean's rage,
Clinging to the wreckage of a splintered life?
What good are hopes of unseen shores,
When swirling waters drag you flailing
Down to hell?
King of Thrace, all debts come due,
Even at the hands of women slaves.

The chorus enters the tent.
Silence.
Then uproar and screams from the tent.

POLUMESTOR

Oh my god… help! Help!
No! You're blinding me!
Children! Where are you ?
Run! Run for your lives!
I am blind. I see nothing.
Children! Oh god no… No!
You filthy demon bitches! You've murdered by sons!

Hekabe emerges from the tent, followed by the other women.

POLUMESTOR

Never… I will never let you escape!

HEKABE

Cry out all you like, Polumestor.
No power on heaven or on earth can bring light to your eyes
    or life to your sons.
As for your revenge on me,
    already you have done all there is to do.

To the women.

You see, the Thracian monster
    finds his way from the tent.
Stay clear of him. He is not yet tame.

Polumestor emerges from the tent,
lunging and scrambling on all fours like a wounded animal,
grabbing blindly after Hekabe and the women with his hands.
His eyes are streaming blood.

POLUMESTOR

Where are you? Murderous hags, I'll find you
    if I have to crawl over every rock in Thrace.
Where are you? You'll pay for this.
I'll hound you to your graves.
Cursed Trojan bitches! Where are you hiding?
I know you're here. Oh if I could only see!
I hear you. I hear your steps. I hear you breathe.
One right lunge and I would drag you to the ground,
        tearing your flesh apart with my hands and teeth,
            glad in the spattering rain of your blood.
I will be sated with each of you. You will make my feast.

Where am I to go?
I cannot leave my children
    to be clawed apart by hellish Bakkhai,
        a meal for savage mountain bitches,
    their carcasses picked clean and left
        to whiten in the sun.
Where? Where am I to go?
Like a ship tacking into port,
    I must go back to that death-sodden lair.
I must shroud and guard my young.

Polumestor finds his way back into the tent.
He drags the bloody corpses of his sons from the tent,
covering them with a cloth he has found inside.
He crouches over the bodies of his sons
as if to ward off any further evil.

CHORUS

Wretched man, you are poisoned from the well
    of your own deeds,
Some god has seen to your undoing with pitiless dispatch.

POLUMESTOR

Help! Help!
Men of Thrace, warriors, bring your sharpened spears.
Come to me!
Greeks! Help! Rescue me, in god's name!
Doesn't anyone hear me? Won't anyone come to me?
Is no one there?

I am the victim of women, utterly ruined by women.
What has happened to me is strange and dreadful
    beyond belief.

Where do I turn? Where do I go?
If I had wings to leap into the sky,
    I would quit this darkened earth
    and soar like a giant moth to the fiery vault of heaven
        until, like a torch, I burst to flame.
Otherwise, I wait even now for the hooded ferryman
    to journey me to blackest hell.

CHORUS

No one can be blamed for wishing to be rid of life,
    when life becomes a burden too heavy to bear.

Agamemnon enters with his guards.

AGAMEMNON

What is all this uproar?
The mountains are alive
    with echoing screams and cries of anguish.
Troy fell with less tumult than this.

POLUMESTOR

Dearest Agamemnon, is that you?
Yes, I know your voice, my friend.
Look at me. Do you see what I have suffered?

AGAMEMNON

What an ungodly sight.
You poor wretch, who has done this to you?
Who has bloodied your eyes
    and left them dense as stones?
Who has butchered your two boys?
This is the work of a hatred I dread to imagine.

POLUMESTOR

Hekabe! It was Hekabe and her hags!
They have destroyed me.
They have worse than destroyed me.

AGAMEMNON

What are you saying?

To Hekabe.

You did this, Hekabe?
This unspeakable atrocity is *your* doing?

POLUMESTOR

You mean that bitch is here, now?

Lunging aimlessly, in hope of grabbing hold of Hekabe.

Where? Tell me where she is.
All I need is one hand on her
    and I'll rip her open like rotten fruit.

AGAMEMNON

Restraining him.

Hold on. What's come over you?

POLUMESTOR

For god's sake, let me go!
Let me have my way with her.
I'm telling you to unhand me.

AGAMEMNON

And I say "no"! Cage this savagery of yours
    and give me your account of what's gone on.
If I'm to judge with any justice in this case,
    I must hear your side of things.

POLUMESTOR

All right, I will tell you what there is to know.
I took in the youngest son of Priamos,
    a boy named Poludoros, sent to me in fear
        of Troy's imminent collapse.
I was to protect and nurture him; but I took his life instead.
This much I admit. It was the only prudent thing to do.

I was afraid, and my reasoning ran as follows.
How could I afford to house the last surviving heir to Troy?
When this child would come of age
    would he not be driven by one dream:
        to resuscitate his race and seek revenge?
And if you Greeks found out about my secret guest,
    would you stand by and let this boy become a man?
No. It was clear to me
    this boy would bring a second Trojan war to Thrace.
And I would rule a land of ravaged fields and smoking ruins.
You see I was hostage to this boy,
    and I freed myself the only way I could.

All was well again…
    until Hekabe found out what I had done.
She lured me here with tales of hidden Trojan gold.
And to avoid unwanted ears and eyes,
    she led me to her tent with my two boys.

Once inside, I sat upon the ground,
    closed in on every side by Trojan slaves.
What then took place was strange but smoothly done,
    too quick to question at the time.
It seemed that everything I brought into the tent
    was made the sudden object of some fuss.
My cloak was held up to the light
    to display its Thracian weave.
My sword and spears were handed around the tent.
Their craftsmanship was held in awe.

The atmosphere was close and warm,
    and I thought it not amiss that I had been relieved
        of my only means of self-defense
    and separated from my sons.
Suddenly, at some unseen signal from their queen,
    the women threw their doting ways aside,
    drew glinting daggers from their robes,
    and slashed the life from both my boys.
I barely saw what happened to my sons
    as I was tackled by a wall of frenzied women
    and hurled upon my back into the dust.
My hands and feet were pinned in place
    by a concerted strength I could not hope to match.
Even when I tried to lift my head,
    they grabbed my hair and wrapped it in their fists,
        slamming my head against the rocky ground.
I was now a victim made ready for their lurid plans,
    spread apart and bawling like a netted beast.
One by one they took their turns with me,
    in acts hideous beyond the reach of words.
Straddling me whose struggles were in vain,
    they plunged into the sockets of my eyes
        the brooch-pins taken from their loosened gowns.
My eyes went dark with a pain I've never known
    and my face became a river running deep with blood.
Their ritual complete, my women captors,
    leaping to their feet, fled the tent
    and ran from my exploding wrath.
Set free from their snares at last,
    I leave a bleeding trail in their pursuit,
        groping and lunging at empty air,
    without a trace of sight or scent
        to guide me to my prey.

Agamemnon, you see the awful price I've paid
    for my simple zeal on your behalf,
        clearing from your path a likely future foe.
Finally it comes down to this.
I am not the first man to take abuse from women,
    nor shall I be the last.
I call upon that consortium of men
    who have suffered much from women at their worst
    to confirm what I have learned today
        to be the simple truth.

No sea nor soil nor womb of any sort yields creatures
  so vile and worthy of our hate as women.

HEKABE

Agamemnon, we would do wrong
  to let a desperate man's loud words
    deafen our ears to the message of his deeds.
Worthy deeds make for worthy speeches,
  but odious deeds plead their case in the basest of terms.
There is nothing worse than rot wrapped in finery.
Behind whatever veil of words, however finely woven,
  a rotten life begins to smell and give itself away.
Cover your ears to the craft of this man's words
  and you will smell the kind of man he is.

Turning to Polumestor.

You say you slew my son for friendship's sake,
  to spare the Greeks a second toilsome war.
But how many favors would it take
  to enamor Greeks of savage Thrace?
More favors than your barbarous mind could conjure up.
And when did you start courting Greeks… and why?
What ties of your blood or common cause
  obtain between you two?
Or *was* it fear that pushed you to the path you took?
This fear is sheer contrivance on your part.
You are transparent in what you've done and why.
You slew my son for gold. He was the victim of your greed.
We would have to be as blind as you've become
  not to see you standing naked in your guilt.
Polumestor, surely you know this:
    if you had proved yourself worthy of our trust,
    rearing our child in safety while he came of age,
      your honor as a man would be intact.
True friendship shines forth most,
  when put to such a test as this.
And in my son you would have had a friend for life,
  sharing his own wealth with you
    should you ever fall in need.
But you took a very different path;
  and, even in your blindness,
    you can see where it has led.
You have your gold and nothing else.
May it bring you happiness and length of days.

HEKABE

To Agamemnon.

To you, Agamemnon, I say this:
If you take this man's side,
    you prove yourself as base as he.
This godless man has betrayed his friends,
    murdered his helpless guest,
    lied and stolen and proved himself
        in every way a villain.
You treat him well, and you are the same as he.
With this, I've said enough.

AGAMEMNON

I have no liking for the place I'm in.
If I judge another's wrongs, it is because I must.
Hearing what I've heard from both of you
    and seeing what I've seen,
    I would live in shame throughout my days,
        if I were now to turn my back and simply walk away.
Polumestor, it seems amply clear to me you killed your guest,
    not as any favor to us Greeks,
        but for the gold you wanted as your own.
All the rest you've said is sheer pretence,
    fast thinking under courtroom pressure,
        nothing more.
To you it seems a slight matter to slay a guest.
We Greeks have very different thoughts in this regard.
What you have done we find contemptible…
    not the sort of fault we overlook.
I would condemn myself in acquitting you.
And this I shall not do.
Since you have unleashed evil,
    you must let it drag you where it will.

POLUMESTOR

Bested by a woman. What a bitter judgement.

HEKABE

You think you suffer too much for what you have done?

POLUMESTOR

My sons… my eyes… you bitch!

HEKABE

You complain to me? You think I suffer less?

POLUMESTOR

Hag, you exult in ruining me!

HEKABE

Would you begrudge me that?

POLUMESTOR

Your triumph will be brief.

HEKABE

It will suffice.

POLUMESTOR

I know more than you suspect.
Dionusos, our Thracian seer,
    has read for me the future like a book.

HEKABE

There must be pages missing in his tome.
Pity he told you nothing of today.

POLUMESTOR

Wretch, mocking me like some superior being!
You shall drown at sea,
    hurling yourself from the masthead of a Greek ship.

HEKABE

I spit your prophecies back into your face.
You see a lot for someone with no eyes.

POLUMESTOR

I see your daughter slain…

HEKABE

Kassandra?

POLUMESTOR

By this king's wife. She keeps a grim house.

HEKABE
Never so mad as that would she be driven.

POLUMESTOR
Mad enough to hack her own husband down
with an axe, while he...

AGAMEMNON
Enough! You've raved on long enough!
Do you want to suffer still another blow?

POLUMESTOR
Play bold now; but a bath of blood
is being drawn for you at home.

AGAMEMNON
Seize him... and drag him off!

POLUMESTOR
My words strike home?

AGAMEMNON
To his guards.

Gag him!

POLUMESTOR
Fair enough. I've said it all.

AGAMEMNON
Waste no time with this man.
Let his own insolence of tongue
entertain him on some desert isle.

Polumestor is dragged off my Agamemnon's guards.

And you, Hekabe,
bury your dead as best you may.

Hekabe leaves with her Handmaiden.

Women of Troy, be ready for our sailing.
I feel a breeze across my face, and it will take us home.

A blessing on our journey now.
May we leave our long miseries behind
　　and find our homes at peace.

Agamemnon exits.

CHORUS

To the tents,
　　to the ships,
　　　　to the lives no longer ours.
This is the way of slaves: to echo others' lives.
When fate stands in our path, it is we who must give way.

The Chorus exits.